Isn't it Wonderful!

Themes from the Bible retold for children

by

A. J. McC

Illustrations by Ferelith Eccles Williams

COLLINS

✠ GOD IS WISE, GOD IS KIND

God is wonderful – he understands everything. He gives us a wonderful world to live in – an exciting world! and there's so much to see in it.

The Reading comes from the book of a wise man called Ben Sirah.

God must be very wise.

He made every grain of sand on the beach
and there's so many of them
that we could never count them all.

He made every drop of rain that falls from the sky
and we couldn't count them all either.

Look up at the sky
and see how high it is above us!

Go up to the top of a high building
and look how far you can see
(and the land stretches even further away still!)

Go out on the sea in a boat
and look down into the water
and see how deep it is!

God is very, very wise,
and he wants all his friends
to become wise like him.

✠

The world is so good that we want to say 'thank you' to God. Here is a poem from the 'Book of Praise' which does just that.

Thank you, Father,
You are good to us.

You made the sky for us
For you are so wise.

Thank you, Father,
You are good to us.

You made the earth for us
For you are kind.
Thank you, Father,
You are good to us.

You gave the sun to us
To shine all day long.
Thank you, Father,
You are good to us.

You gave the moon to us
To shine through the night.
Thank you, Father,
You are good to us.

God is certainly wise, but he is also very kind. In fact he has been very good to all of us, so we must try to be kind to each other, then we will be good like him. This is what Jesus tells us to do.

The Reading comes from the Gospel of Saint Matthew.

One day, Jesus said:

God is your Father,
you must behave like his children.

He takes care of everyone
– bad people and good people
honest people and dishonest people.
He treats them all the same.

Look how the sun shines
and the rain falls
on everyone in the same way.

If you are God's children
you must act like God
and take care of each other.

3

⊠ THE WORLD IS GOOD

God made everything for us and he made it all very good!
The Reading comes from the Book of Beginnings.

God said:

Let there be dry land!
(and he called it 'The Earth').

Let there be water round the land!
(and he called it 'The Sea').

Let there be a roof over the land!
(and he called it 'The Sky').

And God said it was good.

God said:

Let there be a light to shine during the day!
(and he called it 'The Sun').

Let there be smaller lights to shine at night!
(and he called them 'the Moon' and 'The Stars').

And God said it was good.

God said:

Let plants grow in the soil
and let there be fruit trees!

Let there be fishes to swim in the sea
and birds to fly in the sky!

Let there be wild animals and tame animals
and all sorts of creeping things!

And God said it was good.

Then God said:

Let us make people,
and he made men and women
and put them in charge of the world.

Then God looked at everything
and God said 'It is all very good!'

Jesus knew that the world was very good. In fact he liked the world a lot.
He thought it was very beautiful – especially at harvest time.

The Reading comes from the Gospel of Saint John.

One day Jesus said:

Everything is going just right!
There's going to be a marvellous harvest.

Isn't it wonderful!
One man sows the seeds
and three months later the field is full of golden corn,
ready for the harvest.
Then another man comes and cuts down the corn
and stores it in the barns.
And everyone is happy together.

✤ FLOWERS ARE BEAUTIFUL

During the Winter most of the flowers stop growing. But in Spring time they begin to come up once more. Each year it is the same! You could almost say the flowers die away in winter and then rise up again in Spring!

The Reading comes from 'The Song of Songs'.

When Winter is finished,
and the rain has stopped falling,
then the plants begin to grow.

The birds sing
and leaves appear on the trees
and at last you can smell the perfume of the flowers.

This is the time to sing for joy!

✤

The trees look so strong, you would hardly think they changed at all. But they do! Each year they grow new leaves and some trees even grow fruit that you can eat.

This next reading is a poem from 'The Book of Praise' and it's all about some old fruit trees that grew near a river.

Down by the river
Is a good place for trees.
If the water flows near them,
They never grow dry.
Their leaves are not withered,
They stay green and alive.
And each year their branches
Are covered with fruit.

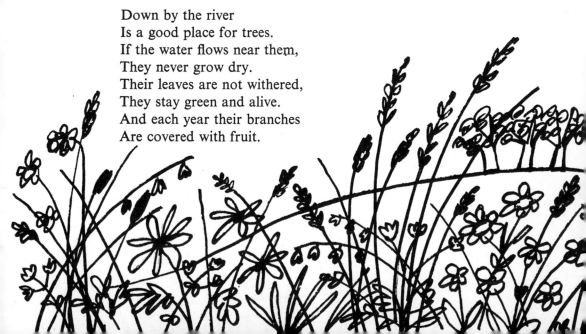

Jesus knew all about plants. He knew how they grow from little seeds that you plant in the ground. The next reading tells a story about some seeds that grew badly and some other seeds that grew well.

The Reading comes from the Gospel of Saint Mark.

One day, when Jesus was down by the sea,
there were so many people around him
that he had to go and sit in a boat
so he could talk to all the people
who were standing on the beach.

One of the stories he told went like this:

'Listen everyone!' he said.

There was once a man who went out to plant some seeds.
As he walked along,
some of the seeds fell on the path
and the birds came and ate them up.

Some of the seeds fell on hard soil,
and they never had a chance.
They had just begun to grow,
when the sun came out and dried them up
– for they had no roots to suck up the water.

Some of the seeds fell on a patch of weeds,
and the weeds choked them
so they couldn't grow properly.

But the man did manage to plant most of the seeds
and he planted them in good soil
just where he wanted.
And they grew and they grew and they grew.

✛ FLOWERS DON'T WORRY ABOUT ANYTHING!

God likes flowers – he thinks they make the world beautiful, and he doesn't want them to be spoilt.

The Reading comes from the book of a Wise Man called Isaiah.

God says:

I am a Gardener,
and I look after my garden
all day and all night.

I keep watering all my plants
because I don't want them to dry up
or their leaves will fall off.

If I find any weeds,
I will pull them up and burn them.

Then the whole of my garden will be filled with flowers.

Jesus liked flowers as well. He knew that his Father took good care of them. That was obvious. But he wanted people to know that God doesn't just take care of the flowers, he takes care of everything – and everyone.

The Reading comes from the Gospel of Saint Matthew.

One day Jesus said:

Look at the flowers!

They don't worry about anything,
and yet they look more beautiful
than a King dressed in his best clothes!

So don't worry about yourselves.
If God takes so much trouble over the flowers
even though they are going to be cut down tomorrow and burnt,
then he will certainly take good care of you.

GOD MAKES EVERYTHING GROW

Harvest is a wonderful time when everyone is happy.
The Reading comes from the Book of Moses.

God said:

If you obey my rules
and do what I ask you to do,
then I will give you all the rain you need,
just at the right time to make things grow.

Everything will grow beautifully in the soil
and the trees will be covered with fruit.

You will be able to harvest your food all the year round
and eat as much as you want.

Jesus thought it was wonderful
to see the corn growing all by itself.

The Reading comes from the Gospel of Saint Mark.

One day Jesus said:

The farmer goes out
and plants the seeds in his field.
But then he leaves them there
to grow all by themselves.

He doesn't understand *how* they grow
– he only knows they do –
even while he is asleep at night.

All of a sudden a little shoot appears
then it grows larger
and then the corn is there
– all fully grown.

Then Jesus said:
That is the way God works!

✥ GOD TAKES CARE OF THE ANIMALS AS WELL

Once upon a time there was a terrible flood and it rained for so long that the whole of the land was covered in deep water.

But God didn't want any of the good people to drown in the floods, so he told a man called Noah to get them all into a boat where they would be safe and dry. Then God told Noah to save all the animals as well for they also had done nothing wrong.

The Reading comes from the Book of Beginnings.

God said to Noah:

Go and find two of each of the birds and the animals
and put them aboard your ship.
Then make sure you have enough food for them
and for everyone else.
So Noah did as he was told
and he took aboard the wild beasts and the cattle
and the animals that crawl on the earth
and the birds that fly in the sky.

The flood was very bad, but it stopped raining in the end, and the wind began to blow all the water away.

Then Noah sent out a raven
to see if the raven could find dry land.
But it just flew round and round in circles
– there was nowhere dry for it to land.

Then Noah sent out a dove
to see if the dry land had appeared again,
and even the dove could not find anywhere to land.

10

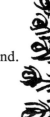

But Noah sent out the dove a second time,
and it came back with an olive branch in its beak.
The next time Noah sent out the dove
it did not come back at all
for it had found dry land at last
and stayed there.

Then God said to Noah:

Come out of your ship
and let all the animals and birds come out as well,
for the flood is finished.

So Noah did what he was told
and he thanked God for saving him from drowning
in the waters of the flood.

In the story of the Flood, the dove brought back a branch from the olive tree. In the next reading, we have one of the stories Jesus told, and this time the birds are resting on the branches of a mustard tree.

The Reading comes from the Gospel of Saint Mark.

One day Jesus said:

The mustard seed is the smallest seed in the world,
but when you plant it in the ground,
it grows and becomes so big
that the birds can come
and build their nests in the shade of its branches.

Then Jesus said:
God works like that.

11

⊠ THE SHEPHERD AND HIS SHEEP

This first reading is all about looking after sheep. Unless we are shepherds ourselves, we will probably not have a lamb or a sheep at home, but we might have some other kind of animal as a pet. This reading tells us to take good care of it.

The Reading comes from the book of a Wise Man called Ezekiel.

Shepherds should feed their sheep.
They should build them up, if they are weak,
and take care of them when they are sick.

If any of the sheep get lost,
the shepherd should go after them
in case they are left out on the cold mountainside
and the wild animals attack them and kill them.

If you are a good shepherd
you must really look after your sheep.

God looks after each of us just as carefully as a good shepherd looks after his sheep.

Jesus is a good shepherd as well and he knows each one of us – even our names. He is certainly not a stranger to us, he is our friend, and we are glad to follow him.

The Reading comes from the Gospel of Saint John.

One day Jesus said:
Sheep listen to their own shepherd
and they will follow him.
He can even call them one by one
for he knows their names
and he can call them out of the sheepfold through the gate.

When they have all come out,
he walks in front of them,
and they all follow
because they know the sound of his voice.

Of course, they would never follow a stranger
because they would not know the sound of his voice.
They would run away from him
if he told them to follow him.

Then Jesus said:

I am a shepherd
and I'm a *good* shepherd.
I know all my sheep, every one of them,
and they know me.

✠ SPARROWS DON'T COST MUCH!

Saint John knew that every father loves his child. Sometimes, when our own father is angry with us for doing wrong, we may think that he doesn't love us and will never forgive us. But that's not true – he's probably quite proud of us, even if he is sometimes angry with us.
Saint John says that God is our Father as well, and he loves us all.

The Reading comes from one of the Letters of Saint John.

Dear Friends,

See how much God thinks of us –
he calls us *his children*
and we really are, you know.

God takes care of us
so we must take care of each other.

God loves us
so we must love each other.

If we don't know that
we don't know anything about God our Father,
because 'God *is* Love'.

Jesus must often have seen the little sparrows hopping about on the ground. But even if they are so small, God still looks after them, because 'God is love'.

The Reading comes from the Gospel of Saint Luke.

One day Jesus said:
God does not forget about even the little sparrows.

They are not very important
and they don't cost much to buy,
but God remembers each one of them.

So don't worry about yourself.
God will take good care of you
for you are worth more than all the sparrows in the world.

LET THERE BE LIGHT!

Sometimes it's exciting to be out in the dark, but usually it's rather frightening. You can't see and you bump into things, and it's scarey! Wouldn't it be terrible if there was no light at all and it was always dark!

The Reading comes from the Book of Beginnings.

In the beginning,
the world was all empty,
and everything was dark and gloomy.
But God was there
like the wind that blows over the sea at night.

And God said:
Let there be light!
And there was light!

And the light was wonderful!

People didn't have electric lights, when Jesus was born. They used candles instead. But the candles did the same job and lit up the darkness.

The Reading comes from the Gospel of Saint Matthew.

One day Jesus said:
Do you light a candle
and then cover it over with a bucket?

Of course you don't,
you want it to light up the whole room
so that everyone can see.

Then Jesus said:
If you are good,
you will be like a candle
that shines brightly for everyone to see.

And if they see that you are good
(and they know that you are following God)
then they will know that God is good.

✷ BLIND MEN CAN'T SEE!

It's good to enjoy the sunshine and the daylight, if you can see. But some people are blind and they cannot see the sun at all. They cannot even tell the difference between daylight and darkness. Jesus must have known how terrible it was to be blind. This reading tells the story of a blind man that Jesus cured.

The Reading comes from the Gospel of Saint Luke.

One day
when Jesus and his friends were leaving Jericho,
a blind beggar heard Jesus going by.
Everyone was saying 'It's Jesus of Nazareth!'
So the blind man shouted out to Jesus and said:
'Help me, Jesus!'
Everyone told him to shut up,
but this only made him shout all the louder.

Jesus heard him shouting
and he stopped.
'Bring him here,' he said.
So they did.
'Cheer up,' they told the blind man,
'Jesus wants to see you.'
Then Jesus said:
'What do you want me to do for you?'
And the blind man said:
'Lord, please let me see.'
So Jesus said, 'All right – you trusted me;
You *will* get better!'

And straightaway, the man could see,
and he was able to walk behind Jesus along the road.

16

It is wonderful to see, and we thank God for it. Here is a prayer of thanks from the Book of Praise. The blind man who came to Jesus might even have said it himself when he was healed.

I love you, my Lord,
for you have made me strong.
I thank you, my Lord,
for you have heard my prayer.

You have been like a light before my eyes.
You have made my darkness into light.

⊡ DON'T TOUCH THE FIRE OR YOU'LL GET BURNT!

If you see a big bonfire burning brightly, you will see how the flames flicker and crackle up into the air. Fire is funny stuff! The flames never stay still – they leap and twist about. And they are so hot that you would burn yourself badly if you touched them.

The Reading comes from the Book of a Wise Man called Isaiah.

It is good to bake bread over a fire.
It is good to sit down in front of it and feel warm.

But the little fire can blaze up
and then no one can bear the heat of its flames,
for it can burn people
as if they were wisps of straw.

Next we have a story about a farmer who burnt all the weeds in his fields in a great big fire.

The Reading comes from the Gospel of Saint Matthew.

One day Jesus told this story:

Once upon a time there was a farmer
who sowed good seed in his field.
But one night,
a wicked man came and sowed *weeds* in the field
and ran away.

The wheat began to grow beautifully,
but the weeds grew at the same time,
and they were all mixed up with the wheat.

So the man who helped the farmer went to him and said:
'Where have all the weeds come from?
I thought we only sowed good clean seed in that field!'

'I think we have an enemy,' said the farmer,
'and he has planted weeds in our field
just to cause us trouble.'

'Shall we pull out all the weeds now?' said the man,

'No!' said the farmer.
'If you do that,
you may pull up all the wheat as well.
No, leave them as they are,
and at harvest time
we will gather the weeds first
and tie them into bundles
and burn them on the fire.
Then we will be able to collect the wheat safely
and put it into my barn.'

Then Jesus said:
That's how God works as well.

✠ THE FIRE OF GOD

*We cannot see God but we still know he is here with us. He is like the
flames of a fire. We can all tell when a fire is burning – even with our eyes
shut. We can feel its heat coming towards us even if we cannot see the
heat. Even if we sit and watch the flames, we cannot see them properly.
They come and go too quickly.*

*Perhaps that is why God is often said to be like a burning fire – because
he is so strong and warm, and yet many people still cannot see him!*

The Reading comes from the Book of Moses.

Moses was a shepherd
who lived near the desert.

One day,
he went up Mount Sinai with his sheep
and he saw a bush that seemed to be on fire.
When he came closer to the bush,
he heard the voice of God coming from the blazing flames.
God said: 'Moses!'
and Moses said, 'Yes, Lord, here I am.'
Then God said,
'I am the God of your family,
the God of Abraham, Isaac and Jacob.

'I can see that the Hebrew People are all slaves in Egypt.
But I am going to help you all.
You will escape from Egypt,
and I will give you a beautiful land to live in
and you will have plenty to eat there.'

*Moses felt that God was like a blazing fire because God was strong.
Jesus is the same. He also is like a fire, which burns so strongly that
everyone can feel his strength and power.*

The Reading comes from the Gospel of Saint Luke.

One day Jesus said:
I am like a blazing fire,
and I want everyone else to feel its heat.

20

HELP, LORD, WE'RE DROWNING!

Here is a poem from the Book of Praise. It was written by a man who nearly drowned. He must have walked into the river or into the sea, and gone too far. He is scared stiff and prays to God for help.

Save me, O God, I'm drowning!
The water is up to my neck!
I'm standing on soft oozy mud
and my feet are beginning to sink.
I cannot stand up
for the waves push me down,
and the water is getting still deeper.

Save me, O God, I'm drowning!
The mud is sinking below me,
the water is pushing me over!
Save me or I will die!

Water is strong and dangerous, that's why we should always be careful in the sea. It's very easy to get drowned. The next reading tells the story of the time when the followers of Jesus thought they were going to be drowned in a storm at sea.

The Reading comes from the Gospel of Saint Mark.

One night Jesus said to his friends:

'Let's go over to the other side of the lake.'

So they left the big crowds
and got into a boat to go to the other side.
Then suddenly, the wind began to blow,
and big waves splashed into the little boat
so that it started to fill with water.

But Jesus was so tired,
he just lay down with his head on a cushion
and went to sleep.

22

His friends woke him up, and said,
'Look! We're sinking.
Why aren't you doing something to help?'

So Jesus sat up
and he told the wind to stop making a noise,
and he told the waves to stop rocking the boat.

Suddenly the wind just died away
and the waves became calm again.
Then Jesus turned to his friends and said,

'Why were you so frightened?
You should have known by now
that I would not let you down.'

Here is another poem from the Book of Praise. The person who wrote
it must have thought that God was asleep – like Jesus in the boat.
Sometimes we may think God has gone to sleep, especially if we
don't get what we ask for. But we can be sure that God is always
ready to help, if we need him.

Wake up, God!
Don't say you're still sleeping!
Can't you see we need you.
So please don't hide away.
Look! We're all in trouble.
Don't forget us, please.

Stand up, God, and hear us!
Show us that you love us.
Come and help us now.

✛ WATER, WATER EVERYWHERE, AND NOT A DROP TO DRINK!

Moses and all the People of God escaped from Egypt. They had been slaves – but now they were free, and they were on their way to 'The Promised Land'. But first they had to cross the desert, and everything became hot and sandy. Then they ran out of water.

The Reading comes from the Book of Moses.

They walked for three whole days,
until they had used up all their water.
But when they looked for some more water,
they could only find a pool
where the water was too horrible to drink.

Everyone grumbled at Moses, and said,
'What are we going to drink now?'
So Moses asked God to help him,
and God did not let him down.

Moses found a special kind of wood
that he could put into the water
to make it nice to drink again.
Then everyone could have as much water as they wanted.

Not very long afterwards,
they came to a place
where there were lots of palm trees
and seven pools of clean drinking water,
and so they pitched their tents there and set up camp.

*Even though the People of God were terribly thirsty, they still could not
drink the water in the poisoned pool, until Moses made it good to drink
again. In the next story, Jesus and his friends were very thirsty, but they
couldn't drink the water because it was right down at the bottom of a deep
well.*

The Reading comes from the Gospel of Saint John.

One day Jesus and his friends had to go from Judea to Galilee.
They walked all through the morning until they were tired,
then they came to a place called 'Jacob's Well'
and stopped there for a rest.

Jesus sat down beside the well outside the town,
while his friends went to buy some food,
and as he sat there,
a woman came along with a jug
to get some water from the well.

Jesus asked this woman for a drink.
At first, the woman was surprised that Jesus spoke to her
because she did not know him at all.
But they soon began to talk to each other
and they were still talking
when the others came back with the food.
And she left her jug behind, when she went away,
so they could all have a drink of water from the well.

⊞ FOOD, GLORIOUS FOOD!

Everyone enjoys eating. Food is one of the best things that God gives to us. In this reading, we hear the story of Abraham's visitors, who came to see him and stayed for a tasty meal.

The Reading comes from the Book of Beginnings.

One day Abraham was sitting in front of his tent.
It was a hot afternoon
and the sun was high in the sky.

When Abraham looked up,
he saw three men coming towards him.
So he got up and went out to welcome them.

'Come and have something to eat,' he said.
'Come and sit down in the shade of the trees
and I will get you some water
so that you can have a wash.'

Abraham then went back into his tent
and told Sarah, his wife, to bake some bread.
Next he told his servant
to go and get some tasty meat and cook it.
And he went himself to get some milk,
so that he could give his visitors a really good meal.

While they were eating, one of the visitors said,

'Tell your wife
that we will come back in a year's time
and she will have a baby.'
Now Sarah was in the tent and she heard him saying this
and she just laughed,
because she was far too old to have a baby.
But later on Abraham came and told her off.
'God can do anything he wants,' he said,
'and if he wants you to have a baby,
you will!'

And, of course, she did.
She gave birth to a little baby boy
and she called him 'Isaac'.

Jesus enjoyed his food and we often hear about him going out for a meal with his friends. In the next reading, he is telling us how to make bread, and he shows us how the yeast makes the flour completely different.

The Reading comes from the Gospel of Saint Matthew.

One day Jesus said:

'When you make bread,
you take a lot of flour
(and some water)
and you mix it all up with a little bit of yeast.

'This little bit of yeast then gets to work on the flour
and it makes it grow and swell up,
until it is all ready for baking.'

Then Jesus said:

'God works like that.'

✠ BREAD FROM HEAVEN

We all need to eat food or we will starve to death. If we didn't eat anything at all, we would soon become weak, and we could easily become ill.
In the same way, we need Jesus or we will become 'starved' and weak in another way, and then we may even start to do things wrong through our own fault.

The Reading comes from the Gospel of Saint John.

One day Jesus said:

My Father gives you 'bread from Heaven'
and this bread will make you good like him.

Then he said:

I am the 'bread from Heaven'. If you come to me,
you will never be 'hungry'.

Yes, I have come to feed you,
and if you eat my food
you will live with me
and I will live with you.

Jesus comes to feed us when we are 'hungry' for him. But it is not ordinary food he gives to us. He gives himself *to us, because he loves us.*

The Reading comes from one of the Letters of Saint Paul.

Dear Friends,
At the Last Supper before he died,
Jesus took some bread, saying,
'Father, thank you for giving us this bread to eat.'
Then he broke it up into pieces and said,
'This is me – this is my body.
This is my gift to you.
Remember me,
when you do this in future.'

Later on when the meal was finished,
Jesus took a cup of wine and said,
'This is the cup of friendship
that is filled with my love.
Remember me
when you do this in future.
'Whenever you eat this bread and drink this cup,
let everyone know that I died
for you because I love you.'

✶ IT'S GOOD TO HEAR AND GOOD TO SPEAK

If we could not hear anything or if we couldn't say a single word, life would be very dull! Jesus knew this, so he went out of his way to help people who were deaf and dumb.

The Reading comes from the Gospel of Saint Mark.

One day a man came to Jesus
and he was deaf
(he couldn't speak very well either).

Someone asked Jesus to bless this man
so Jesus told him to come away to somewhere quiet
where there wasn't such a crowd.

Then Jesus touched the man's ears
and put his finger on his tongue,
and said a prayer.

Suddenly the man said, 'I can hear!'
– and he could speak much better as well.

All the people were astonished to see what Jesus could do,
and they said,
'Everything he does is wonderful.'

Perhaps the deaf man who was healed said a prayer like this.
The Reading comes from the Book of a Wise Man called Isaiah.

I want to tell the whole wide world
– 'God has been good to me!'
I want to tell the whole wide world
– 'God is wonderful!'
I want to sing and to shout
because I am so happy
for God has come to me
and he is great!

☒ THE SOUND OF GOD

*God is powerful and strong, but he is also kind and gentle. This reading
tells us about this gentleness of God for, as Elijah discovers, God can be as
gentle as a whispering breeze.*

The Reading comes from the Story of the Kings.

Once upon a time there was a man called Elijah
who had an argument with the King.
The King was very angry with Elijah
and Elijah had to escape as fast as he could.
So he tucked up his cloak
and ran away.

Elijah was so frightened
that he went off into the desert
and walked for the whole of a day as far as he could.
Then he sat down under a little bush and said,
'Please let me die, Lord,
I've had enough!'
Then he fell asleep.

When he woke up, he had something to eat and drink
and he felt a lot better.
So he began to walk again
until he came to Mount Sinai,
and he stayed that night
in a cave on the mountainside.

Then God told him to listen very carefully.

First the wind began to blow
and it blew so strongly
that the big rocks came crashing down
and smashed themselves to pieces in the valley below.

But Elijah couldn't hear the voice of God.

Then the mountain began to shake with an earthquake.

But Elijah still couldn't hear the voice of God.

Then a fire broke out on the mountainside,
and the flames from the fire
leaped up into the sky with a loud crackle.

But Elijah still couldn't hear the voice of God.

Then suddenly,
everything became very still,
and Elijah heard the sound of a gentle breeze,
and he shut his eyes
for at last he *could* hear the sound of the voice of God.

Jesus could also be very gentle and he wanted his friends to be gentle with each other. Then they would live in peace.

The Reading comes from the Gospel of Saint John.

One day Jesus said,

'I leave you "PEACE".
I give you my own kind of peace.

'Do not be worried or upset.
do not be afraid.'

✥ MAKE MUSIC AND PRAISE GOD

Music can make us happy and when we're happy, we praise God much better.

The Reading comes from one of the Letters of Saint Paul.

Dear Friends,

Don't forget that God wants to get to know you,
because he loves you.

But you must help each other
to know how much God loves you
by singing his songs.

And remember!
When you sing these songs,
say 'thank you' to God
for he is your Father in heaven.

God likes to hear people when they are happy, and the people in the next poem from the Book of Praise are very happy.

God is very good to us
   Let's praise him.

Let's play the trumpet
   Let's praise him.
Let's play the guitar
   Let's praise him.
Let's play the drums
   Let's praise him.
Let's play the violins
   Let's praise him.
Let's play the recorders
   Let's praise him.

Let's crash the cymbals
  Let's praise him.
Let's dance for joy
  Let's praise him.

Let everyone who can breathe praise God!

Jesus had not been in Jerusalem for quite a long time. So when he did come back his friends were very glad to see him and, of course, they showed their happiness as soon as they began to sing.

The Reading comes from the Gospel of Saint Luke.

When Jesus arrived at the Olive Hill,
a crowd of his friends came out to meet him.
They were very happy,
and began to praise God at the top of their voices,
thanking him for all the wonderful things that Jesus had done.
And they started to sing an old song
that began like this:

'Glory to God in the highest,
and peace to his people on earth.
Blessed is he who comes in the name of the Lord!'

Collins Liturgical Publications
187 Piccadilly, London W1V 9DA

Collins Liturgical Australia
PO Box 3023 Sydney 2001

ISBN 0 00 599787 9

First published as part of *Listen!*, Collins 1976
© text 1976 A. J. McCallen
© illustrations 1976, 1984
William Collins Sons & Co Ltd.

This edition, first published 1984

Printed by William Collins Sons & Co Ltd, Glasgow